Retail Loss Prevention

Theft Prevention Made Easy

Matthew D. Thomson

3/22/2015

This manual has been designed to give retail managers the tools that they need to detect and prevent theft within their retail establishments.

Introduction.

This manual has been designed as a tool for retail managers to use as a guideline for theft management and loss prevention. I am confident that there is something to be learned in this manual that will in fact save you money and time. If used properly, the methods in this book will no doubt assist you in the controlling of your inventory and cash flow. Located in the back of the book you will find several forms that you may use to help you in the battle against theft.

The manual has been broken down into several main groups:

1. Hiring
2. Employee Theft
3. Methods of Stealing
4. Prevention
5. Vendor Theft
6. Paperwork Errors
7. Shoplifting
8. Robbery Prevention
9. Blank Forms

These areas will all be covered extensively and I will break down the main areas of concern that you need to be aware of.

Here is the disclaimer - For as long as people have been selling items, there have been people trying to figure out how to get them for free. Theft detection is an ever-evolving process that moves along with technology advancements. For every discovery, a new method emerges that is even harder to detect. This manual will not cover every possible method of detecting theft but will cover the basic tools that you will need to detect theft in your own retail establishment.

The Hiring process

The hiring process is probably one of the most critical aspects to loss prevention. As retail managers, we look for honest, hard working, dependable staff to help us run our businesses. Selecting the right employees makes a bigger difference than you might think in the success of your business. Your employees are, after all, the face of your company. They represent you and what you stand for to the public every day.

But, how do we get honest, hard working people to apply? Sadly, we as managers have little control over who chooses to apply to come and work for us. However, we do have the control to pick the right candidates from the pool of applicants. In this section, we will cover some of the basic tools that you can use to assist in selecting the right applicant.

Let's begin with a review of the application itself. If you have ever filled out an application before, you will notice that from company to company, they all want pretty much the same information. There is a reason for that. Over hundreds of years, retailers have developed a system that will ask information that is telling of a potential applicant. As a retailer, you just need to learn how to interoperate their answers.

Job History

Let's begin with job history. When reviewing an applicant's job history, you need to look for red flags. These red flags are: Gaps in employment, short tenure with multiple employers, the unwillingness of the applicant to release consent to contact, and failure to fill out the address or phone number for an employer. Let's review each of these red flags individually.

> **Gaps in employment**: If an applicant has gaps of periods for which they are not employed, you will want to ask yourself what possible reasons there are for those gaps. There can be legitimate reasons for the gaps like childbirth, relocations, schooling, or others. However, there can be far more sinister reasons as well such as imprisonment, lack of motivation in finding employment, drug use, etc.

> **Short Tenure**: If an applicant spends only a few weeks to a few months at multiple employers, you need to ask the question, why? Short periods of employment might be an indication that the applicant has learning deficiencies, they may be unmotivated (lazy) or a series of other problems.

Another possible cause for this is that the applicant is desperate for money and will leave a potential career for an increase in hourly wages or salary. Be cautious of this type of applicant!

Can we contact: This is a common question on most applications. When an applicant doesn't want you to contact a previous employer, there is usually a pretty good reason for it. The most common reason is that they are not sure what the employer will tell you about their performance or reason for separation. Be very cautious of any applicant that doesn't want you to talk to their previous employer. Ask yourself what they are trying to hide?

Omitting Information: Just like not giving permission for you to contact their previous employer, omitting information or providing false information can be another way of preventing you from finding out the truth about your applicant. Another common method is to put that the business closed and there is nobody to contact.

Many companies have moved to an electronic application process. Those that have usually ask applicants for an email address during the application process. If you have access to your applicants email address, I urge you to look at it as part of the review process. You can tell a lot about an applicant based off of what they chose for their personal email.

For example, BillSmith79@xyz.com I can speculate that Bill Smith was born in 1979 based off of his email. That alone gives me more information than I would have had without that email address.

Another example would be an email address that reads ILoveMyKids420@mydomain.com With this email, I can tell that the applicant has children and there is a drug reference in the address as well. 420 is a universal code for marijuana.

Some of the hidden codes in email addresses that you should be on the lookout for are listed below:

- 187 - Police code for homicide
- 420 - Universal code for marijuana
- 69 - Sexual reference
- Look for random misspelled or abbreviated words like H8TR (Hater) as in CopH8TR@xyz.com

The Interview

The interview process is your one chance to learn more about a potential employee before entrusting them with your business. The interview process gives you a glimpse into the person and may be the greatest chance that you have to get to know your applicants. Asking the right types of questions can make all of the difference.

When interviewing a potential employee, you will want to ask open-ended questions. An open-ended question is one that cannot be answered with a simple yes or no answer and will force the applicant to explain in more depth. Asking these types of questions will often reveal more that you would suspect they would and will give you more information to use when making the decision to hire or not.

An example of a close-ended question would be: "Have you ever worked retail before?" to which the applicant can give either a yes or no answer to satisfy the requirement of the question. These types of questions give you little information at all to use in your decision to hire or not.

An example of an open-ended question would be: "I see on your application that you worked at XYZ Company, What were your job duties there?" to which the applicant has to answer in more detail to satisfy the question.

But before we can get to the questions that you should ask, we need to cover what you cannot ask. Several US laws have been set to prevent discrimination amongst employers. Because of this, there are several areas that you need to avoid when interviewing a potential employee. If an applicant volunteers information, that is perfectly acceptable and up to them. However, there are questions that you cannot ask your applicant.

Do not ask questions about the following topics:

- Race
- Religion
- Sexual Orientation
- National Origin (Nationality)
- Birthplace
- Disability
- Marital or Family Status (including children)
- Political Views and Associations
- Alcohol, Tobacco and Drug Use
- Military Discharge
- Height and Weight

Asking questions about any of the items listed above could be considered grounds for discrimination should the applicant not receive the job. We will want to avoid directly asking any of these types of questions. At the end of this Manual is an interview guide that will list several predesigned and open-ended questions that you can ask. When interviewing your applicant, it is a good idea to record their responses to the questions on the form provided for later review.

Some examples of the types of questions that you should ask are:

1. Why are you interested in a position with our company?
2. How many years of retail experience do you have?
3. Tell me about your experience with handling cash?
4. In your own words, what is good customer service?
5. Tell me about a time that you gave good customer service on the job.
6. Give me an example of how you handled a customer complaint in the past.
7. Are you currently working and if so, why do you want to leave your current job?
8. What do you consider your greatest accomplishment at your last job?
9. What do you consider your biggest weakness?
10. How would your previous supervisor describe you?
11. If hired, do you have reliable transportation to and from work?
12. What is your availability? Can you work overtime if needed? Weekends?
13. What outside activities are you involved in that would interfere with your scheduling?
14. This position pays $----- per hour. Does that meet your financial requirements?
15. What can you tell me about yourself that I cannot learn from reading your application?

After the Interview

A trick that I learned after many years of conducting interviews is whenever possible, walk the applicant to their car after the completion of the interview. A glimpse inside an applicant's car can tell you a lot about a person. An applicant will typically dress up and put their best foot forward during an interview but don't think to clean out their car beforehand.

When you look in the applicants vehicle, look to see if they are a clean and organized type of personality or if they are unorganized and disheveled. Look for key items in the vehicle that will tell you a little more about their personal lives without you having to ask for it. If there are empty beer cans on the back seat of the car next to the child seat, you may have just learned a few important facts about your candidate. If they get into the car and have to blow into an interlock breathalyzer device to start the car, that might tell you something more about who they are as well.

EMPLOYEE THEFT

In a recent study, It was discovered that and estimated 47% of retail losses are due to employee theft. That's right, almost half of all losses that your business will incur will be at the hands of your employees. Below is a chart from a survey taken by National Retail Security in June of 2007

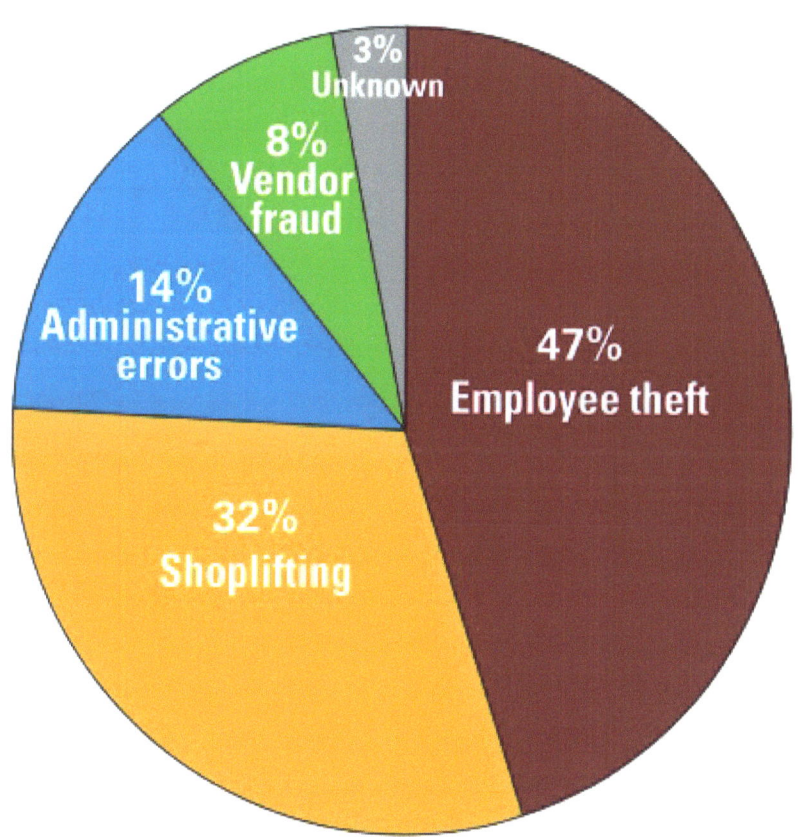

Sources of Shrink
Total employer losses: $41.5 billion

3% Unknown
8% Vendor fraud
14% Administrative errors
47% Employee theft
32% Shoplifting

Source: National Retail Security Survey, June 2007

It has been my experience that the strongest tool against theft is the conception that someone is looking for it. The fear of being caught is both a motivator and a deterrent so this method may not always work for everyone. For some, the thrill of not being caught or eluding discovery is a way for them to live out a more exciting "James Bond" type of lifestyle. Through my experience, I have found that in about 20% of the cases that I have studied, the need for money was not the motivator. It was the "Thrill of the chase" in not being discovered as a thief or in other words, "getting away with it". However, the remaining 80% of cases are motivated by the need for money. In the back of the book you will find a worksheet called The Theft

Triangle. We will cover this worksheet in more detail in the prevention section of this manual. This worksheet will help you to identify your main suspects by reviewing the three main areas of theft. These areas are: The need for money, the opportunity to get the money, and the general attitude of the employee. It is strongly suggested that you as a manager complete an employee evaluation of each employee on a regular basis. Not just when you suspect theft. If you have skilled employees stealing from you, you may not notice the subtle signs that they leave behind.

When an employee begins to steal there is typically a pattern that will form where the employee will try several different methods of stealing before they find the one that will work for them the best. Usually the employee will start with small amounts and eventually work their way up to larger amounts. This is known as escalation and it usually isn't until the employee has evolved their pattern that they are detected. During the initial period of theft it is imperative to detect the loss before the employee reaches the next level of escalation in their theft. As the employee progresses, they will typically find one method of theft that works for them and slowly perfect it as to make it more difficult for you to detect. The longer they go undetected, the more you will lose and the harder it will be for you to detect.

A typical thief may start out with something as small as a dollar a day, after realizing that they can get away with that amount without getting caught, they will escalate their pattern to five dollars a day. If that works, greed will take over and the periods of escalation become shorter and the amounts begin to get larger. By the time that you start to suspect that there is a problem, you have already lost much more than you think you have.

METHODS OF STEALING

There are several methods that employees may use to steal your money. In this chapter we will cover most of the known methods, however it is important to remember that if there is a will there is a way. Keep in mind that there may be other methods used by the employee that have not been covered in this manual. It is also important to keep this information to yourself. If your employees know exactly what you are looking for, they will also know where you are not looking. Remember - Where there is a will, there is a way.

1. THE OPEN TILL. This method is where the cashier simply does not make any attempt to process the transaction through the cash register. The cashier will take the money and place it into the register and use one of the following methods to track how much of the money in the till has not been accounted for and needs to be taken out before closing. The money that is in the till that needs to be removed is referred to as a "pad". This is where the term "padding the till" comes from. However there have been many instances where the employee will take the money out of the register or till and place it in the pocket immediately after the customer leaves. One of the most common ways to do this is to simply tell the customers that the register is "broken" and you cant ring it up right now. The cashier will then take the money and place it into the register. You may notice that the cashier does not completely close the register drawer as many registers require a sale to open the drawer. If the register does not close before the customer walks away from the counter you may want to watch the cashier closely. Most cashiers are faster than the customers and if the cashier hesitates there may be a reason for the hesitation, usually theft.

As an exercise, ask each of your employees the cost of several of your most commonly purchased items, then ask them the total amount with tax. You will probably be surprised to find that many of your employees have the totals memorized already. No, this does not mean that they are all thieves, it just shows you how easy it is to steal.

> Example: Your cashier, John, is standing at the till waiting for the next customer to come up. The customer approaches the register and has in his hand a 32-ounce fountain drink. John, having rung up thousands of fountain drinks before knows that, tax included, the cost of the drink is equal to ninety-five cents. John proudly tells the customer his total without ringing the drink into the register. The customer hands john a crisp $1 bill to cover the cost of his purchase. John taps a few buttons on the register to make it appear as though he is ringing up the transaction and opens the drawer with the "no sale" or "Safe Drop" buttons, hands the customer a nickel for change and places the dollar bill in

the drawer. John has just successfully stolen $0.95 from you and the customer is none the wiser. But now John has a new problem, he needs to remember that he needs to take that money out of the register before he closes his shift.

2. VOIDS AND NO SALES Most companies have set up a way for you to track how many voids and no sales your cashiers have. While nobody expects that your cashiers are infallible and couldn't have a legitimate reason to hit no sale or void, these are very common ways for your employee to steal. If you remember the scenario above with our cashier, John, you will remember that John had to open his drawer to give the customer his change back. The no sale that John pushed to open the drawer can be tracked through the register system.

As a manager, you should be on the lookout for patterns to arise that point in the direction of theft. If John has an average of 23 no sales for each of his shifts, that would be a HUGE red flag. It's your job to detect these patterns as they emerge.

Voided items are another way for the cashier to steal from you. Just like the no sales, you should watch for patterns to develop with the use of voids. The cashier will ring up all of the customer's items and usually leave the most expensive item to be the last item rung up. The cashier will tell the customer the total for their purchase and then void out the last item before cashing out the sale and collecting the money from the customer.

Example: It's your cashier, John at the register again. This time the customer comes up and has a bottle of water, a candy bar and asks for a pack of cigarettes. John quickly realizes that the pack of cigarettes has the most value so he will ring those up last. John rings up the candy bar followed by the water and then finally the pack of cigarettes. He tells the customer that his total is $9.04 and the customer hands john a ten-dollar bill to pay for his purchase.

Without the customer noticing, John very quickly voids out the pack of cigarettes only and hits cash on the register. He gives the customer his .96 cents and places the ten in the drawer. John knows that the pack of cigarettes with tax comes to $4.97 each. That means that he just stole $5 from you. While the candy bar and bottle of water were correctly processed, the cigarettes were not.

It's a good idea to develop some sort of spreadsheet for your store. Use this spreadsheet to track how many voids normally happen on each of your shifts. You will be able to find a trend that begins to develop.

3. MARKERS. Markers are small items used to track the amount of money that needs to be taken out of the till before the shift close. This is an easy way for the employee to keep track of the "Pad" in their registers. The items are assigned a dollar value by the cashier and used to track the theft in dollar amounts. For example the cashier may place a penny on the top of the register for every dollar that he has stolen. A nickel would represent five dollars, a dime would represent ten dollars and so forth. This does not have to be money markers, the same concept can work with a variety of items such as paperclips, matches, buttons, etc. In addition, the markers do not need to be placed on the top of the register, they can be placed to the side, in the extra slot in the register drawer, and sometimes in the pocket of the employee. Placing the markers in the pocket of the employee will make it much more difficult for you as a manager to detect. However if you notice the employee placing unusual items in their pocket or continually counting the change in their pocket, that should raise a red flag for you.

Another common marker is the use of a penny dish or "floater money", money that the cashier claims is for customers who don't have enough. Often times the cashier will use this money as their marker. It is strongly suggested that if you have a penny dish you dispose of it and discourage any further use. Instruct the cashiers that if the customer is a few cents short to let them have the item. It is far better to be several cents short on each of your shifts than to have a thief taking much more money from you.

This method is common amongst employees that wish to minimize the risk of getting caught taking money directly from the register and putting it in their pocket. If they can keep adding to the pad in the drawer, they will only need to take it out at the end or close to the end of their shift once and effectively reduce their chances of being detected when they take the money.

> Example: John, our cashier from the examples above, has effectively stolen a dollar from the last customer that he helped. However, John doesn't plan on stopping at just a dollar. He needs to get more money and is concerned that if he takes it out of the register after each time he steals, somebody is going to notice. That wouldn't be good for John. John decides that he is going to keep track of his money with visual markers. Then, at the end of his shift, he only has to take money out of the till once. John places a penny on the top of the register to remind him that he has a dollar in the till that is his. Now, each time that he steals, he can just add another penny to the top of the register. At the end of his shift, John has three pennies, a nickel and a dime. He knows that he needs to take out $18.00 from his till before he closes it. If anyone asks about the extra change on top of the register, it will be easy for John to explain that a customer left his or her change behind. Who would be suspicious of eighteen cents?

4. TALLY SHEETS. Tally sheets are small scraps of paper usually found around or inside the cash register. These sheets will have numbers or scratches on them indicating how much money has been stolen by the cashier. These are also used by the thief to keep track of the pad that needs to be removed from the register. These sheets are useful tools to in remembering to remove X amount from the cash register at a later time. This is a common tool used by thieves because of availability and ease. This eliminates the problem of having to remember an amount and chance forgetting a number. However, a good thief will commit his total to memory and not leave "evidence" on a scrap of paper. An example of common tally sheets would look similar to one of the following illustrations.

12	39
14	15
26	54
11	6
37	60
2	
39	

In this illustration, the cashier adds 12 + 14 to get 26. Then 26 + 11 to get 37 and so on until he gets to 60 indicating the need for him to remove $60.00 from the register and place it in his pocket.

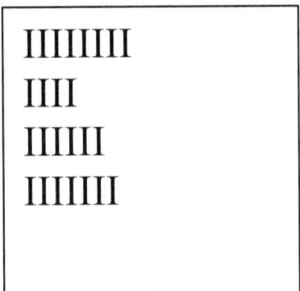

In this illustration the cashier is using "Chicken Scratches" to tally his Theft. Typically, one scratch for one dollar. This illustration indicates a theft of $25.00.

5. CALCULATORS. Calculators are the modern form of a tally sheet. They work in the same manner but are easier and quicker to use. Calculators seem to be the favorite of most thieves simply because of the convenience. Customers typically do not tend to be concerned if they witness a cashier using a calculator. Most major companies have adopted various policies preventing calculators from being placed within arms reach of any register. This is just good practice. As a deterrent, casually clear out all of the memory on all calculators as you walk past them throughout the day. Next time you hear "I'm sorry sir but my register is down right now, let me just add up your total." you should think twice about what the cashier is actually doing.

6. VISUAL BLOCKING. Visual blocking is one of the easiest theft tracks for customers to notice. Visual blocking is when objects such as posters, notes, displays, and other large objects are placed in the windows of the retail establishment. This is done in an effort to limit the view of the cashier from the street. This eliminates the threat of someone watching them from across the street with binoculars. This action however also inhibits the ability for police and local law enforcement officers to view the inside of your establishment while passing in their vehicles. Again, many large companies have adopted policies preventing the placement of any object in the windows. As a rule of thumb, no more than 25% of your windows should be blocked with advertisements.

A common tool for the thief in visual blocking is donation Plaques. Donation plaques are the little paper balloons, Shamrocks, hearts, etc. that customers put their name on when they donate money to a worthy cause. These plaques are then placed on the walls and windows of the business to let all of the customers see them. More times than not I have seen them on the windows directly in front or behind the cashier. If you use these, suggest to your employees that they are placed on the walls but not on the windows.

Another all to common use of the visual blocking method is when the cashier will turn the customer display screen away from the customer or place something in front of the screen to block the customers view of it. These screens are normally strategically placed on the registers to allow the customers to have a visual confirmation of the amount they are being charged. A dishonest cashier will typically turn the display screen from the view of the customer and charge them slightly more than the total purchase amount. Most customers will not say anything due to the fact that they are trusting that the cashier knows what he or she is doing. If possible, affix the display unit to a stationary item to prevent it from being turned. Another deterrent is to place signage on your register to alert the customers to ask for a receipt for their transaction. Or a sign saying, If you do not receive a receipt please contact a member of management for your "free item". This will make the cashier know that the customer will be looking. Setting up your cash register to automatically print a receipt at the end of each transaction is the best way to ensure each customer gets one.

7. PIG LISTS. Pig lists or pig sheets are an easy way to steal but usually do not add up to large amounts. Many companies will allow their employees to consume food and beverages and use what is known as a pig sheet. This sheet keeps track of what the employee has eaten and the employee pays another cashier from this list at the end of their shift. More often than not I have found that pig sheets tend to end up in the trash and not get paid for. Individually this may not cost you more than $5.00. However, five dollars times 5 days a week times 4 weeks(month) is equal to $100.00. If you are currently allowing your employees to use pig lists I would strongly advise you to stop. As a general rule, items should be paid for before they are consumed or used and a copy of the receipt should be taped to them.

8. GRAZING. Grazing is one of the most common methods of theft. Grazing is just what it sounds like. Your employees consume a variety of food products inside your store without paying for them. This can be a bag of chips, a candy bar, a sandwich - whatever they are hungry for at the moment. Many employees feel that this is the least a company can do for their employees and don't even consider this "theft".

Ask yourself one question, have you ever consumed something at work that you failed to pay for, whether it was intentional or not? Have you ever taken a pen home? Do you know anyone who has? Grazing is far more common than you would think because people view it as miniscule. A little theft won't hurt a company this large. Right? Big companies like this expect that there will be a little bit of theft. That's why the prices are so high. Right? You might be surprised at some of the justifications that I have heard for this type of theft.

Grazing can take place many different ways. You need to be as creative in discovering it as they are in doing it.

> Example: John is working his normal shift at the convenience store. As part of his normal shift duties, John has to stock the roller grill with fresh hot dogs. He's only supposed to put three of each type of hot dog on the grill because that's what his manager wants. The problem is, John is hungry but didn't bring enough money to buy anything to eat. John loads the grill up with 5 of each of the dogs and waits until the end of his shift so that he can take home the "wasted" products from the grill that didn't sell during his shift. They would have thrown them out anyway, right? This isn't really theft is it?

9. HELPING FRIENDS. This is when friends of the cashier are invited to come into the store and are allowed to "graze" or consume anything they can eat before leaving. Although this may not seam to be the greatest threat, small amounts add up to be big ones over time. Another way to accomplish this is to arrange with a friend earlier in the day to come in and purchase several items. The cashier then waves the item in front of the scanner, being careful to not actually ring up the item, and places it into a bag. After several items have been placed into the bag, the cashier will take the last item (usually the least expensive) and actually ring it up, charge the customer, and make the change due. The customer (the cashiers friend and accomplice) has now left the store with several items having only purchased one. This method is mainly to avoid being caught on camera. It is more of a rehearsed event than a spontaneous one.

One of the ways that the cashiers can get the money or "pad" that they have stolen out of the register without being caught is to have someone else carry it out. To accomplish this you have to have a friend that you can trust.

Example: A Customer (your cashiers accomplice) walks into the store, gets a pack of gum ($.79) and takes it to the register. At the register the cashier takes the gum and scans it. The cashier totals the sale ($.84) and accepts $1 from the customer. The cashier then counts out $153.16 and hands it to the customer saying have a great day and come back soon. The customer leaves with the change from their purchase as well as the pad from the cashier. The cashier goes on to help the next customer.

The customer just removed $153.00 of the cashier's money (his pad). They will undoubtedly meet after the cashiers shift and exchange the money. Now that the money is safely out of the store the cashier does not have the worry of being caught taking it out of the register or of being caught with the money in his pocket. Now, if confronted, all the cashier has to say is "How could I steal when I don't even have any money on me".

10. SWEETHEARTING - This method of stealing is also known as collusion. Sweet hearting is when your cashier(s) allow their friends or regular customers to come in and take product without paying for it. This happens far more that you may realize that it does.

Every store - No matter what you are selling has a regular base of customers. These are customers that come in every day and frequent your store more than normal customers do. I'm sure that you can think of the first names of several of your location's "regular" customers.

Over time, your cashiers and possibly even yourself develop a working relationship with these customers. You know about their lives, their children and everything in between. These customers are the bread and butter of your business and your sales wouldn't be the same without them. They are quite possibly the sole reason that your business is still open. That is, when things go as planned.

Because your cashiers have developed a personal relationship with these customers, they tend to make them deals that they normally wouldn't for any other customer. Ask yourself if you have ever heard one of your cashiers tell a customer "It's on the house today" or "It's on me".

Example: There's good old John back at the register. Let's face it, he's not your best employee. In walks one of your regular customers, Bob. Bob comes in every morning for a cup of coffee and a newspaper. He has come in every morning at exactly six AM for the last three years and purchased the exact same thing. Chances are, he's going to continue doing that for many years to come. He's so regular that you could set a clock by him.

Bob get's his normal cup of coffee and his newspaper and comes up to the counter. He and John engage in the same small talk that they do every morning and when done, Bob moves to the register to pay for his items. John quickly waves him off stating that this one is on the house. "You spend enough money here already" says John with a chuckle.

In the example above, your store just lost the cost of a cup of coffee and a newspaper. Not a big deal in and of itself. However, that adds up quickly when it happens every day. It adds up even faster when you have multiple employees doing it.

It's highly unlikely that these customers or friends will come in and tell you that they are getting free product when they are the ones that benefit from it. You will need to be on the lookout for the signs that this is happening at your location. However, it is not uncommon for these customers to complain when they do get charged. They come to expect that they will not be charged after this type of behavior continues for long periods.

11. EARLY CHECKOUT If you have a cahier that always counts out and closes his or her till early, there may be a reason behind it. Early checkouts are one of the warning signs that you as a manager need to be on the lookout for. If your cashier is checking out early, it may be so that they can remove their pad from the register before the next shift comes in. This makes it easier to remove the money from the register without being detected. The less people that are they're watching what they are doing, the more success he will have.

12. FAKE ROBBERY I know that it may seem unheard of, but if you remember that desperate people take desperate measures, it's not implausible that someone fake a robbery. A robbery would ensure that the employee gains the entire contents of the register. One of the largest tip off's that a robbery would be fake is in the amount of money that is gained by the robber. If your cashier has more in the till than they should have had, there may be a reason for it.

Example: Your cashier, John is at it again. But this time, he needs even more money than normal. Last night he came home from work to find an eviction notice on his front door because he's behind three months on his rent. On top of that, he can't even afford to feed his five-month-old child. I know, my heart goes out to him too! After all, he's such a standup guy!

Most people would go out and get a second job to make the two ends of their budget meet. Not John! That would be too much work for him! So, John devises a plan and with a little bit of help from one of his friends, he'll be back on top in no time! John and his friend Steve devise a plan to stack the register with money and then Steve will come in and "rob" the place. John won't call the police or the manager until Steve has gotten far away with the money. They can meet up later and split the spoils and nobody will be the wiser.

Like most businesses do, there are limits as to how much money you john can have in the register before he is forced to drop it in the safe. That won't be a problem for John because he can do the drops and just keep the money in the register rather than put it in the safe. That's what most of the employees do anyway. Right?

In the example above, the store looses all of the money in the register and the drops that the casher held outside of the safe. That could add up to a lot of money to lose all at once. And nobody ever suspects the cashier.

One thing that you can do to help prevent this type of thing from happening is make sure that all recorded drops are immediately placed into the safe or secured wherever your company does that. Also, set limits for how much money can be kept in the register at one time. Most modern registers have setting that will prompt the cashier to drop money once a preset level has been reached. Keeping the temptation down may help eliminate the fake robbery method.

Prevention

Now that you know some of the methods that are used to steal your money and merchandise, lets cover some of the best practices that you as a manager can perform to help detect and even prevent these issues. In retail, there is a common perception that your employees will respect what you inspect. If they know that you are watching, it will be much more difficult for them to steal from you.

THE THEFT TRIANGLE

As a manager, it is a good idea to evaluate your staff periodically. Remember that there are typically two reasons that people will steal from you. 1. They need the money and will do anything to get it. 2. They thrive off of the thrill from not being caught.

It is harder to determine who your thrill seekers are because there are rarely any warning signs. For the individuals that steal out of necessity, it is a little easier. Using the theft triangle as a guide when evaluating your employees might make it easier for you to know which employees are at a higher risk.

The theft triangle covers three behaviors that most of the "need it" thieves will exhibit: Attitude, Need and Opportunity.

The worksheet works on a scoring system. The higher the number, the more likely the employee is to be a thief. Each of the three areas is scored from 1 to 5.

Attitude: This section describes the general and overall attitude of the employee.

    1- employee has a great attitude.

    2 - Very good attitude.

    3- Good attitude.

    4- Mediocre attitude.

    5- Poor attitude.

Need: This section is for the need of the employee to acquire money.

    1- No need

    2- Little need

    3- Average need

    4- Substantial need

    5- Great need.

Opportunity: This section covers the opportunity that the employee has to steal.

    1- Little to no opportunity.

    2- Little opportunity

    3- Average opportunity

    4- Substantial opportunity

    5- Lots of opportunity

When completing the worksheet, use a form similar to the one below and put all of your employees on it. When you are done with all of your employees, total up their score to see which employees have the highest score. Employees with the highest scores are the ones that you will want to pay attention to first.

Employee Name	Attitude	Need	Opportunity	Total

A copy of the Theft Triangle worksheet is included in the back of the manual so that you can make copies and use periodically for your store.

While the theft triangle is good at directing your attention to the problem employees, it should not be the only thing that you use. There are many other things that you need to check on a regular basis, things like void counts, no sale counts, till audits, periodic checks of the transaction detail reports, etc. We can discuss some of these in more detail.

One of the best ways to catch an employee that you think is stealing is to do a surprise till audit on them. Most modern register systems have a method for the manager to do an in shift audit. If your registers do not have this functionality, you may simply need to close the shift and have the cashier reopen a new shift when you are done.

As I stated before, one of the best deterrents of theft is the conception that someone is looking for it. Regular inventory audits, shift audits and transaction audits will help more than you think they will.

Based off of what we have learned already, below is a checklist of things that you can do to help maintain the integrity of your employees.

1. Clear out the calculators in your store as you walk past them. - Remember that a thief may be using it to keep track of their pad. It's a good idea to hit clear each time you walk past one.
2. Be on the lookout for spare change on the tops of the registers or nearby the registers. It's a good idea to get rid of the "Take a penny - Leave a penny" cups that most stores have by the registers.
3. Be on the lookout for tally sheets. Remember that a thief may use tally sheets to keep track of their pad.
4. Count your inventory - Remember that people will respect what you inspect and are less likely to steal from a category that you are monitoring.
5. If you have video surveillance at your location, try to set aside time each week to review the recorded video. It does no good to have video if you never watch any.
6. Complete surprise cash audits on your cashiers often. You might be surprised what you find.
7. Visit your stores when you normally would not be there. If you work in the morning, Visit at night.
8. Review your cashier statistics every day! Look into voids, refunds, price overrides, no sales, etc. You may actually need to research what happened.
9. Properly train your cashiers. Many of the mistakes that they make on the registers may actually be costing you money. While it may not be intentional on the part of the cashier, you still loose that money. Proper training will help with more efficient and accurate transactions.

Vendor Theft

Vendor theft only makes up 8% of total retail losses. However, this can still add up to a crippling amount of money over time. But, how can your vendors be stealing from you?

A vendor typically does not deal with cash but with merchandise coming into your store. In a typical situation, a delivery truck will arrive at your retail location and will deliver product to your business. After the delivery has been carefully checked in, the driver will deliver an invoice to the store and the invoice will be submitted for payment. No cash has changed hands at this point. Depending on how the vendor conducts business, the invoice is usually due for payment within a specific amount of time. This process has been set up this way to prevent the exchange of cash at the time of the delivery.

So, with that process in place, how do your vendors steal from you. The answer, the only way that they can – they steal merchandise.

Let's start with a simple example. Let's say that one of your vendors stops at your store to deliver a new shipment of chips to you. Your delivery person is Jacob and he has been delivering chips to your store for the last ten years. All of your employees know him and he has a good report with all of them.

Jacob wheels all of his product into the store and puts it right in front of the shelves where his product will be displayed. Jacob then asks your cashier to come over and check him in. Your cashier holds the invoice in his hand and Jacob counts off what is inside all of his many boxes. Once Jacob and your cashier have finished checking off the merchandise, Jacob begins his job of putting the product away on the shelves.

Once all of the product is put away, Jacob wheels his cart full of empty boxes out of the store and he is on his way. What your cashier did not see is that Jacob did not completely empty some of those boxes. When he wheeled out his cart, several of the boxes still had product remaining in them. Your cashier also did not notice that when he was checking off the invoice, the product that Jacob said was there, really was not.

But why would Jacob want to steal his own product? There are several different reasons why this could happen. 1 – He is planning on taking them home. 2 – He is planning to sell them for cash at one of his cash accounts. 3 – He is planning to sell them elsewhere.

There are a few things that you can train your employees to do to help prevent vendor theft.

1. When vendors bring product into the store, ask them to bring it into a neutral area that is not by where their product is displayed. Doing this will prevent the delivery person from taking live

product off of the shelf and putting it into the box to be checked in. You would end up paying for product you already own.

2. Train your employees to touch count all inventory. A vendor should never count his or her own inventory off to you. Your employees should touch count it to make sure that it is really there.

3. Instruct your vendors that all boxes and trash need to be broken down flat before they are removed from the store. Do not let them take out boxes that are not broken down because they may not be empty.

4. Watch the vendors when they are in your store. Vendors typically have access to back rooms and storage areas of the store as well. You never know what goes missing when they have free access without being monitored.

Paperwork Errors

Most employee errors and paperwork errors are honest mistakes made by honest employees. However, paperwork errors still make up 14% of your stores total losses. That adds up to a lot of cash that your retail store is losing.

Below are a few things that you can do to help reduce the amount of paperwork errors that happen at your store.

1. Train your employees. Training your employees to properly use the cash register and POS (Point of Sale) equipment is essential to your success. When your employees complete a transaction at the POS properly, the amount of errors made diminish quickly.

2. Make sure that your employees are trained to always count the change back to the customer. Doing this will make it less likely that the customers are handed back too much or not enough change for their transactions.

3. Make sure that everything in your store is properly priced. Mispriced items may be costing you more money than you think.

4. If using a scanner, make sure that all of the items are in your price book correctly. A simple error in your price book could cost you thousands of dollars over time.

5. Properly and accurately record, monitor and account for all waste items in your store. If you see that you are wasting 24 hot dogs a day, make an adjustment to the number that you are putting out for sale.

6. Use the calculator to do even simple math. Many people claim that they can do math in their head. This is how mistakes are made.

7. Periodically review invoice entry. When invoices are entered into your inventory system, mistakes can be easily made and overlooked that end up costing you money.

Shoplifting

Shoplifting is a major part of retail losses. There are a few things that you can do to help prevent this type of loss in your location. Although you will never be able to stop 100% of shoplifting, you can take some steps to help reduce the amount of loss.

Below are some simple steps that you can take:

1. Greet your customers. If customers know that they are noticed, they are less likely to steal from you.
2. Train your staff to be alert. Be aware of what is going on in the store and not just sitting behind the counter reading a book.
3. Keep your windows to the store open and clear. If people can see in, so can the police. Your customers are less likely to steal if they think that they can be seen.
4. Never leave your customers alone in the store. That's an open invitation for them to take whatever they want.
5. Ask lingering customers of they need help. A lingering customer may simply be waiting for the right chance to steal without being noticed.
6. When ringing up high value items, make sure that you do not place them within the customers reach until after you have collected the funds for the merchandise. All too often, thieves will take the first opportunity to grab the item off of the counter and run out the door without paying.
7. Train your employees to be able to detect counterfeit currency. The Secret Service has printable literature on their website that will tell you what to look for. Visit SecretService.Gov to view their training materials.

Robbery Prevention

Any time that cash is present, the threat of robberies is as well. Robberies are an unfortunate and unavoidable hazard that one has to face when in retail. However, there are some steps that you can take to help minimize the risk.

1. If your company uses them, train your employees to always wear their nametags. It has been proven in multiple studies that robbers are more violent with unnamed victims that with the one with whom they know their first name. Nobody wants to rob Suzie but they have no psychological connection with an unnamed employee.

2. Keep your front windows clear. Sure, all of the signs in the window provide your customers the all of the detail of the sale that you're running and they bring people in off of the streets. Those signs also provide cover for a would be robber. Remember, if they can be seen from the street, they can be caught.

3. Keep the cash in your registers low. Many times, a robber will stake out the store they are planning on robbing beforehand to see if the risk is worth the reward. They will make a small purchase with a large bill to see if the cashier has troubles making change. If they don't have any issues making change, that tells the robber that they will get at least enough money to break a large bill. Many modern register systems will allow you to set a maximum amount that can be in the register.

4. Train your employees to not stand behind the sales counter when not helping a customer. If nobody is there, your cashers should be out on the sales floor keeping busy. A robber has the goal of getting in and out of the store as quickly as possible. If your cashier is already in place behind the register, it makes them a better target.

5. Make sure that your video surveillance system is always working. Many retail establishments even put up stickers or signs letting customers and employees know that they are being recorded. A quick search on the internet and you should be able to source many different styles of stickers that you can use.

6. Whenever financially possible, have multiple employees scheduled. The presence of more people is a deterrent to many thieves.

7. Train your employees beforehand what to do and expect should they be robbed. Training on how to properly respond may even save a life.

What to do in the event of a robbery

1. Remain calm. A robber will mirror your excitement level. If you are overly excited, nervous or emotional, the robber will respond to your emotional level.

2. Comply fully with the demands of the robber. Do not argue with them. Remember, their goal is to get in and to get out as quickly as possible.

3. Let the robber know of any other people on site. "Jennie is in the back room". If Jennie were to walk out of the backroom and surprise the robber it would not be a good thing.

4. Try to gather as many details as possible. You will need this for the police report that you will make later. Look at the details of the robber and try to commit them to memory.

5. Immediately after the robbery, call the police. You will also want to lock the front doors and any witnesses to stay until the police have arrived.

6. Call your direct supervisor. They will want to know what happened as soon as possible.

7. Let the police know anywhere that the robber may have touched. This makes fingerprint recovery possible.

8. Talk to your manager about company provided counseling. Remember, it's ok to be afraid and shaken up.

Blank Forms

Interview Questions

Applicant Name:

Interview Date:

16. Why are you interested in a position with our company?

17. How many years of retail experience do you have?

18. Tell me about your experience with handling cash?

19. In your own words, what is good customer service?

20. Tell me about a time that you gave good customer service on the job.

21. Give me an example of how you handled a customer complaint in the past.

22. Are you currently working and if so, why do you want to leave your current job?

23. What do you consider your greatest accomplishment at your last job?

24. What do you consider your biggest weakness?

25. How would your previous supervisor describe you?

26. If hired, do you have reliable transportation to and from work?

27. What is your availability? Can you work overtime if needed? Weekends?

28. What outside activities are you involved in that would interfere with your scheduling?

29. This position pays $----- per hour. Does that meet your financial requirements?

30. What can you tell me about yourself that I cannot learn from reading your application?

31. The Theft Triangle worksheet works on a scoring system. The higher the number, the more likely the employee is to be a thief. Each of the three areas are scored from 1 to 5.

Attitude: This section describes the general and overall attitude of the employee.

   1- employee has a great attitude.

   2 - Very good attitude.

   3- Good attitude.

   4- Mediocre attitude.

   5- Poor attitude.

The Theft Triangle

Attitude   Need

$

Opportunity

Need: This section is for the need of the employee to acquire money.

   1- No need

   2- Little need

   3- Average need

   4- Substantial need

   5- Great need.

Opportunity: This section covers the opportunity that the employee has to steal.

   1- Little to no opportunity.

   2- Little opportunity

   3- Average opportunity

   4- Substantial opportunity

   5- Lots of opportunity

When completing the worksheet, use a form similar to the one below and put all of your employees on it. When you are done with all of your employees, total up their score to see which employees have the highest score. Employees with the highest scores are the ones that you will want to pay attention to first.

Employee Name	Attitude	Need	Opportunity	Total